Sapiensish: Developing a common language for whole human being (Homo sapiens) by simplification of modern English

---

Johnson K. Gao

The first press of the re-edited version.

jkxgao@gmail.com
ISBN: 978-1-387-58461-1

Published by e-Pollination Inc., company, February 2018.

Sapiensish: Developing a common language for whole human being (Homo sapiens) by simplification of modern English

Johnson K. Gao

Dallas, TX, USA

Dedicated to my wife Catherine W. Gao and my two sons Alvin W. Gao and Raymond F. Gao for their thoughtful initiation and extensive supporting on my work – Sapiensish.

Table of Contents

Sapiensish: Developing a common language for whole human being (Homo sapiens) by simplification of modern English*

Johnson K. Gao

I. Introduction

Language is a tool to deliver one individual's thought or idea or feeling to other individuals through certain kinds of medium, such that sound, image, gesture, touching, motion or even chemicals. In human being the speaking with tongue and mouth and written words or signs by hand are two main forms of language. However, broadly to say, languages also include ultra sonic wave transmission in dolphin, birds' singing, crickets' wings vibration, bees' flying pattern, ants' chemical markers on their trails, blind man finger-touching books, music sheets and performance with instruments – the music language, flag language, light-signal language, telegraphic code, computer language, etc.

The criteria to judge the quality of human languages shall be evaluated by its speeding in speech, area-using efficacy in calligraphy, accuracy in meaning expression, easy understanding, and logic consistency, plus acoustic beauty and visual enjoyment.

Internet needs a globally acceptable language that is simple, accurate, fast in writing/typing, easy to understand, and abundance in message delivery per unit of area (written form) or per unit of time (speaking language), and logical consistency and perfection.

English, Russian, Spanish, Chinese, French, German, Arabic and Japanese are eight leading languages currently used by the majority of human population in the world. Chinese is most popularly used language among world population. While English is the most studied second foreign language in the world among those eight dominate human languages. Chinese language is a Hieroglyphs and difficult to learn.

---

* The first version was called as "Singlish". It was posted on inter net, yahoo.com group, in October 2001. Later, I found that "Singlish" could cause confusion with Singapore local English, which was also called as "Singlish". The second version was modified and posted on scribd.com, in January 2005. The third version was modified on August 14, 2012 and self-published. The forth version was modified on February 2, 2015. This is the fifth version by changing "Siglish" to "Homo Sapiensish, or, Sapiensish, or, HS" with re-editing.

English is a phonetic language and relatively easy to learn. English might be more qualified to be developed into a whole human being common language for typing and show on computer screen. Its basic structure could become a strong candidate or frame with which a globally acceptable language can be developed.

However, English is not perfect. There exist some intrinsic shortcomings in English. It needs to be improved. Certain rules or regulations in English grammar have to be reset: Such as 1. Some English words are spelled differently from their pronunciations (non-phonetic spelling). 2. Articles reduce speeding. 3. Verbs have regular and irregular forms without good reasons, or, logically inconsistency. 4. Most of verbs need to add "s" for the third person, which could be omitted to save time. 5. Letter "s" in plural form of nouns could be omitted as well without causing too much confusion.

The word "Homo Sapiensish", or, "Sapiensish", or, “HS”, stands for "simplified English" to be used as a common language for Homo sapiens. Sapiensish is based on English but it is not English. It is a new international language under development. It is simplified by applying some new rules and regulations, which may be somewhat contradictory to the traditional English. The idea to develop Sapiensish is to create a new language that is easy to learn, fast in typing, and quick to be understood. It could be especially meaningful for international communication on the worldwide web sites.

Languages developed from their simple forms to complex forms. But, now, in the computer age, the world has been shrunken smaller, the complex form of language needs to be reduced to the simplest form that improves exchange of ideas faster. The best international web language should be somewhat symbolic and it permits the clearest and the shortest form or even mathematic symbols as long as other people can get the meaning quickly and correctly. For an example, the symbol “@” had been almost like a dead key in the past, but now it becomes a very popularly used key for sending e-mail. The screen of computer is rather limited in size. So, a web language should use as less space as possible, while it contains as much information as possible. Thus, the idea of one individual can be recognized very fast by people from different corners of the world, despite of what kinds of their mother-tongue languages they had been using. Sapiensish helps brain processing information quicker and to let other people understand faster. So, it has to omit some un-essential components in the English language.

The mynah bird and the parrot will imitate the human language. But, they may not know what they are saying. The dog cannot speak human language. But, the dog could be trained to know the words and act according to the master's instruction. If the owner says 'sit' to his dog, it crouches. Some orangutans, elephants and pigs can be trained to draw paintings, or write words. But, they may not fully know what they mean. All that is because of the imperfection in the neuromuscular connections between the vocal organs and the listening organs. Only human can do that function perfectly.

In certain extent, we could say that human being is a slightly leg behind than certain animals in inheritance of their common “language”. The bird's eggs cannot sing songs. However, some singing birds can sing beautiful songs without learning. The dog cannot speak human language. But, dogs may have their own international "language" (sound). Such as "Woul-woul-woul" is dogs' common “language”, which means "pay attention!" or “I will fight with you!” and its "Grwooh----" sound means "I am angry!" The cat's "Me-Aau" means intimating to its owner and its "Heghl---" sound means "I am angry!" Crickets have no vocal cords and no ears. However, the male cricket has two wings, that can be erected and rub to each other to make a sound, "Geeyuu-geeyuu-geeyuu". The male cricket sings its song all the night telling the female crickets "I am here. I am here." That is called as phonotaxis. And when two male crickets meet together, they will fight. The winner cricket will make several continuous fast sounds - "Geeyuu-geeyuu-geeyuu, geeyuu-geeyuu-geeyuu-geeyu---" announced - "I am the winner!" Before their courtship and mating, the male cricket sends out a voice, or courtship song, like "Jih-jih-geeyu-geeyu-geeyu---" to the female cricket, saying, "I love you!” Whether an America cricket or Asian cricket, they use the same common international cricket “language”. The female cricket is a dumb. However, the female cricket has sound receiver on its joints of the front legs, and the female cricket can understand the male cricket common language's meaning very clearly. To invent an all human being mutually understandable language is actually to reduce the distance that we were leg behind some animals.

One of the unexplored biological researches is how the instinct acquired and inherited through heredity mechanism. The sperm is so tiny. The chromosomes are even much smaller. What is the mechanism that the acquired complicated behavior can be written in to the chromosomes? How could it pass over to the offspring? The nymph of dragonfly lives in fresh water. When it goes through metamorphosis and turns into an adult dragonfly, it can fly without need to learn. That is instinct. One can image that from evolutionary process the ancestor of dragonfly must had gone through inter-species that had diligently learnt how to fly and gradually developed the flying organs and the nervous system that can control the flying muscles. Every instinct must has its heredity governed organs evolution as well. When an infant was born, the first thing is to cry. That is also a kind of instinct. The background of crying is that the infant must have lung, which was not air-filled in the mother’s womb, and tongue, which had already with nerve distribution. And both lung and tongue structures are inherited. If learning language belongs to a kind of acquired behavior, and behavior could be inherited, then, after Sapiensish be practiced by whole human being for generations and generations, it would not be impossible that when an infant was born, instead of crying, it may say; “It’s cold, Mom. Please give me some clothes.” That might be the in-expected benefit of using a universal human language.

Since inter net opens to worldwide people, a universal language has to absorb any good things from worldwide language pool. We have to use scientific rules to govern and transform English. Let it become a more effective tool in human communication and thought exchange. Like in biology, the descendent derived from hybridization is always superior to those derived from inbreeding. I believe that a kind of hybridization language shall be better than an isolate and still language.

There are five simple rules to begin with, which will be listed in the text below. People all over the world are invited to join the Sapiensish development procedures.

Readers are encouraged to discuss and make contributions to set up new rules and new regulations as long as they can simplify the not logic parts of living English.

Sapiensish does not belong to any nations or any races. It is a treasure of mankind, although it has more components/root-words being used in the traditional English. It shall absorb any good essences from any existing languages, such that Chinese, Spanish, Russian, Arabic, French, German, Japanese, etc., should those stuffs can improve Sapiensish. Our aim is to save time and speed up accurate communication. If one person can save three minutes from Sapiensish vs. English per day, which is quite possible and easy to realize, the accumulated save of time by the world population should be 21 billion minutes, which was calculated based on the estimated figure issued by two organizations that the world population had reached 7 billion on October 31, 2011 and March 12, 2012, offered by the United Nations Population Fund and United States Census Bureau, separately. We know that there are 525,600 minutes in a year. 21,000,000,000 minutes divided by 525,600 minutes/year = 39,954 (years). That number further divided by 2012 years, it produces a figure of 19.86. That means the timesaving by the world population per day equals to approximately 20 times that Jesus was born till today. You can feel how significant it could be to apply Sapiensish. My second version of Simplish posted at

http://www.scribd.com/doc/1001/Singlish

That had attracted many visitors.[†]

[†] From 1/1/2007 to 8/15/2012 that site has been visited 28,076 times. The highest peak of the daily count was 847 on 5/23/2009. The second high was 372 on 2/11/2008. The third high was 177 on 11/20/2007. The forth high was 156 on 6/23/2007. A Ph. D. student had asked me to give permission to him to use that article for his thesis defense. That site will be closed when the forth version goes to public.

Five steps will be applied for Sapiensish promotion:

1. Set up few general rules and try them. Don't be worried about critics from doctrinaire or stubborn scholars. We would rather pick up the spirit of a Chinese slogan set by the famous politician and teacher Mr. Mao Ze-dong: "造反有理", which means in English: "To rebel is justice!" Sapiensish permits those seemingly mistakes in current English. On the contrary, we shall purposely design some alterations to fit our purpose, as long as those changes will be favorable to a faster expression and an easier to understand.

2. Encourage people to suggest more new rules or regulations and discuss the benefit to use of those rules. Don't feel to be ashamed in making mistakes in English for those whose mother language is non-English. On the contrary, any structures in the currently used English, if they may cause common mistake by non-English speaking people, shall be re-evaluated. That kind of mistake only means nothing but they might be non-logic to the majority of human being in a larger scale of population. The more frequent mistake it makes, the more urgent need to have them be corrected.

3. Announcing certain rules as fixed formal rules. Let Sapiensish and English counter exist.

4. Produce some sample articles written in Sapiensish and put the English aside. Let people compare if Sapiensish is scientifically superior to English and to see if Sapiensish can practically save of time, space and energy.

5. The critical part for promotion Sapiensish is to form a journal called "Journal of Sapiensish", either in the printed form or a web site, where people can discuss or write articles to express their bright thoughts.

II. Five suggested principal rules and sub rules

1. If a word's written form is different from its spelling form in English, change the written form and let it be in conformed to the pronunciation of that word. Reason: Most written forms in Russian words, or even in English, are pronounced as they are spelled. Why not change those non-phonetic written words? Suggested samples: Change "island" to "iland". (Save 1 letter/6 letters or 16.6 %.) Change "often" to "ofen". (Save 1 letter/5 letters or 20 %.) And you may find much more samples by yourselves.

2. No irregular verbs. There are about 372 irregular verbs in English according to a web page
http://www.englishpage.com/irregularverbs/irregularverbs.html

They are difficult to remember by non-English-speaking people. It is unreasonable to have variety forms of verbs without rules. Please read one sentence to see how confusing English is: "I wash and cut an apple and eat it now." (Present tense) "I washed and cut and ate an apple yesterday". (Past tense) In the later sentence, if people use the word "cutted" or "cuted" instead of "cut", and people use the word "eated" or "eat" instead of "ate", and people use the word "wash" instead of "washed", English people will consider that is wrong. In the above sample, verbs in standard English are contradictory to each others without good reason. Don't you think that English has mental problem? (Smile!) We have to insist on "Every Word Was Created Equal". Why worldwide people have to waste time to learn bad logic and follow the English minds? We should welcome Sapiensish!

Since there are 49 irregular verbs (beat, beset, bet, bid, burst, cast, cost, cut, fit, hit, hurt, knit, let, misset, offset, preset, proofread, put, quit, read, rebid, recast, recut, refit, reread, reset, retreat, retrofit, rewed, rewet, rid, shed, shit, shut, sight-read, slit, spit, split, spread, sublet, thrust, typecast, typeset, underbid, undercut, unset, upset, wed, and wet), which are about 13 % of total irregular verbs in English that are permitted to be used in the same written form for both infinitive (present tense), past tense, and past participle tense without causing any misleading in English, and it is even more true to all Chinese verbs (without need to change forms in different tenses, which had been used for several thousand years with no problem), we suggest that all other irregular verbs and all regular verbs shall follow that rule, i.e. no change form in all verbs. Please share the privilege of the word "cut" with every verb.

Samples in English:

(1) He draws a picture with a pen.

(2) He drew a picture yesterday.

(3) That picture had been drawn for many years.

Expressed in Sapiensish:

(1) He draw picture with pen.

(2) He draw picture yesterday.

(3) That picture have be draw for many year. (Note: If "a" (in English 1, 2) is an article, it can be omitted; "have" and "be" are irregular verbs (refer to text 2.1 and 2.2 below). They do not need change forms in Sapiensish.)

2.1. Hince "be" is an irregular verb, it should be simplified.

Samples in English: [Present tense/past tense/present (past) perfect tense]

(1) I am. I was. I have (had) been.

(2) You are. You were. You have (had) been.

(3) He (She or It) is. He (She or It) was. He (She or It) has (had) been.

(4) We are. We were. We have (had) been.

(5) They are. They were. They have (had) been.

Expressed in Sapiensish: [Present tense/past tense/present (past) perfect tense]

(1) I be. I be. I (have) be.

(2) You be. You be. You (have) be.

(3) He (She or It) be. He (She or It) be. He (She or It) (have) be.

(4) We be. We be. We (have) be.
(5) They be. They be. They (have) be.

2.2. Since "have" is an irregular verb in English, it does not need to change cases in Sapiensish.

Samples in English: [Present tense/past tense/present (past) perfect tense]

(1) I have. I had. I have (had) had.
(2) You have. You had. You have (had) had.
(3) He (She or It) has. He (She or It) had. He (She or It) has (had) had.
(4) We (You or They) have. We (You or They) had. We (You or They) have (had) had.

Expressed in Sapiensish: [Present tense/past tense/present (past) perfect tense]

(1) I have. I (already) have. I (once) have.
(2) You have. You (already) have. You (once) have.
(3) He (She or It) have. He (She or It) (already) have. He (She or It) (once) have.
(4) We (You or They) have. We (You or They) (already) have. We (You or They) (once) have.

Note: People may add "already" before the verb "have" for past tense, such as "You already have"; add "once" before the verb "have" for present perfect tense and past perfect tense, such as " They once have", when they feel that it can better express a specific occasion. But, these two specification words can be omitted.

2.3. Since "do" is an irregular verb in English, it does not need to change cases in Sapiensish.

Samples in English: [Present tense/past tense/present (past) perfect tense]

(1) I do. I did. I have (had) done.
(2) You do. You did. You have (had) done.
(3) He (She or It) does. He (She or It) did. He (She or It) has (had) done.
(4) We (You or They) do. We (You or They) did. We (You or They) have (had) done.

Expressed in Sapiensish: [Present tense/past tense/present (past) perfect tense]

(1) I do. I do. I (have) do.
(2) You do. You do. You (have) do.
(3) He (She or It) do. He (She or It) do. He (She or It) (have) do.
(4) We (You or They) do. We (You or They) do. We (You or They) (have) do.

2.4. Omit suffix "ed" in the past tense and present perfect tense and past perfect tense of all regular verbs in English.

The verb "cut" and "put" in past tense and present or past perfect tense used the same form "cut" and "put". These are commonly used verbs.

Samples in English:
(1) I always cut apples with that small knife.
(2) I cut grass in my yard yesterday.
(3) I have cut the tree before they come to my house.

Since above three sentences did not cause confusion with the word "cut" in English in different tenses, why we must change tenses in all regular verbs by adding "ed"? The "ed" in verb past tense and perfect tense must be allowed to be omitted in order to save time. The omission of "ed" should not be considered as a mistake. Actually, all Chinese verbs do not change forms in past tense and perfect tense. That does not cause confusion in Chinese literature. The Chinese had produced many immortal documents, articles and literatures, among them we just mention one book - "The Art of War" by Sun Wu Tsi (Sun zi), which was written more then two thousand years ago. That book is still understandable in Chinese characters and that article including all verbs can be actually translated in to English, and that book is even studied by Pentagon. We can safely accept the rule - no change in verb form in different tenses.

English samples:
(1) The farmer who plants corns in that field is my brother.
(2) The farmer planted soybeans last year in that field.
(3) The farmer had planted a lot of trees before last summer.

Sapiensish forms:
(1) Farmer who plant corn in that field be my brother.
(2) Farmer plant soybean last year in that field.
(3) Farmer (have) plant a lot of tree before last summer.

3. Omit the "s" for plural nouns. The ending "s" for a plural noun carries no meaning. In English, one people, ten people, a million people are correct forms. If someone used ten peoples, it will be considered as a mistake. You can realize that ten people equal to ten peoples, since ten means plural already. But, if someone used ten boy (omitted "s" in boys), it will be considered as a mistake. Why? Since in "ten boy", the "ten" already means plural, as it is in ten people. So that "s" is no need. Why we need treat things unfairly and to consider that ten people is correct (is the right form), but ten boy is incorrect form? If you are wise, you will say ten boys is a wrong form. In Chinese language all the singular nouns and plural nouns are the same forms. Therefore, the "s" as a suffix after a noun adds a lot of extra work with very little value. Omit that "s" In Sapiensish.

Samples in English:
(1) There is one orange on the table.
(2) There are twelve oranges on the table.
(3) The horse has four legs.

Samples in Sapiensish:

(1) There be one orange on table.
(2) There be twelve orange on table.
(3) Horse have four leg.

4. Omit the "s" for verb form of third person in present tense. The differences between 1st, 2nd, and 3rd person cause certain verbs to change forms.

Samples in English:
(1) I go. You go. He goes. She goes. It goes. They go. We go.
(2) I eat. You eat. He eats. She eats. They eat. We eat.

Suggestion: 3rd person, singular should behave like 1st and 2nd persons in Sapiensish.
(1) I go. You go. He go. She go. It go. They go. We go.
(2) I eat. You eat. He eat. She eat. It eat. They eat. We eat.

5. Omit article(s). Article decorates a noun. It can be omitted without problem.

Samples in English:
(1) He has a boat in the lake near by.
(2) I saw an airplane flying in the blue sky.
(3) The fox is the natural predator of rabbit.

Clearly, here "a", "an" and "the" add no additional meaning to sentences. Consequently, to make sentence short and more solid, we suggest using article sparingly in Sapiensish.

Example in Simplish:
(1) He have boat in lake near by. (Save 3/25 letters, or, 12%)
(2) I see airplane flying in blue sky. (Save 5/32 letters, or, 15.6%)
(3) Fox be natural predator of rabbit. (Save 6/28 letters, or, 21.4%)

III. Practice in writing

Without practice everything is in vain. The author who had declared Sapiensish had tried to re-write the famous fairy tales by Hans Christian Andersen (English version) in Sapiensish. Sample A is a fairy tales - “The Little Match Girl” translated in Sapiensish from English vertion. Sample B is the original form of “The Little Match Girl” in English. The original version has 4,482 characters in English. When that story was written in Simplish, it reduces to 4,042 letters. That means that it can save 440 letters in typing with Sapiensish, or, it is 9.81% less than the original English. Suppose that you can understand the story written in Sapiensish, both you and the writer save nearly 1/10 of the valuable time. Here is another sample of similar practice that I know. To save spaces in printing, more than twenty years ago, some smart meeting organizers had encouraged authors to submit their papers to the proceedings (symposium publication) to omit articles "a" and "the" in Figure legends for illustration of photographs and drawings. They had created a sample in advance for the simplification of English in scientific books. But, Sapiensish has aimed higher and is preparing to make one big leap forward in simplification of English systematically. We hope that Sapiensish will benefit worldwide non-English speaking people, and for the long run, Sapiensish shall also benefit to the English-speaking people.

IV. Conclusion and prospection

Language is always under change day by day. No language can avoid "no change". This had been verified to be true by billions of people in every living language. English is under quick change in the current world. The more people to use English, the faster change it will be. Nowadays, more people can understand that "foto" means "photograph", "u" is the simple form of "you", "i" equals to "I" to avoid using the shift key in typing, "pls" is the shorten form of "Please" in cellular phone text message sending, etc. But, language is always under slow motion of its change. So, we could not expect that Sapiensish can get a drastic transformation overnight. This declaration calls on people all over the world to try and to find good things in their mother languages that can improve English whatever possible; to create something new and correct what is wrongly expressed in the current English. Our activities and scientific practices can force English to yield. We have one aim - to get rid of un-reasonable structure in English and to create a novel universal language - Sapiensish for the realization of a fast, accurate common language for worldwide communication.

Since we know that languages are always under slowly but constantly changes, we have confidence to reach our goal. But, we will not be in a hurry. To find non-phonetic words and to correct them will be much easier than to simplify verbs and tenses. So I call on readers, if you have time you can help us to pick up those non-phonetic words under the letter in dictionary, which is the first letter of your surname, then, post it to our web site.

An old Chinese saying: "If everyone picks firewood, the flame of a camp fire could burn higher". Yes, if more people will join with us and contribute something to Sapiensish, we can work out a complete table to correct most commonly used non-phonetic words in English for our Sapiensish. Also we hope that you can use your merit in your mother language to find some way to improve Sapiensish, verbs and tense, etc. Let the unique human being's common language mature faster.

V. Sample A: Sapiensish form of "The Little Match Girl"

Most terribly cold it be; it snow, and be nearly quite dark, and evening - last evening of year. In this cold and darkness there go along street poor little girl, barehead, and with nake foot. When she leave home she have slipper on, it be true; but what be good of that? They be very large slipper, which her mother have hitherto wear; so large be they; and poor little thing lose them as she scuffle away across street, because of two carriage that roll by dreadfully fast.

One slipper be nowhere to be find; the other have be lay hold of by urchin, and off he run with it; he think it would do capitally for cradle when he some day or other shall have child himself. So little maiden walk on with her tiny nake foot, that be quite red and blue from cold. She carry quantity of match in old apron, and she hold bundle of them in her hand. Nobody have buy anything of her whole livelong day; no one have give her single farthing.

She creep along trembling with cold and hunger - very picture of sorrow, poor little thing!

Flake of snow cover her long fair hair, which fall in beautiful curl around her neck; but of that, of course, she never once now think. From all window candle be gleaming, and it smell so deliciously of roast goose, for you know it be New Year's Eve; yes, of that she think.

In corner form by two house, of which one advance more than other, she seat herself down and cower together. Her little foot she have draw close up to her, but she grow colder and colder, and to go home she do not venture, for she have not sell any match and can not bring a farthing of money: from her father she will certainly get blow, and at home it be cold too, for above her she have only roof, through which wind whistle, even though largest crack be stop up with straw and rag.

Her little hand be almost numb with cold. Oh! match may afford her world of comfort, if she only dare take single one out of bundle, draw it against wall, and warm her finger by it. She draw one out. "Rischt!" how it blaze, how it burn! It be warm, bright flame, like candle, as she hold her hand over it: it be wonderful light. It seem really to little maiden as though she be sitting before large iron stove, with burnish brass foot and brass ornament at top. Fire burn with such bless influence; it warm so delightfully. Little girl have already stretch out her foot to warm them too; but - small flame go out, stove vanish: she have only remain of burn-out match in her hand.

She rub another against wall: it burn brightly, and where light fall on wall, there wall become transparent like veil, so that she can see into room. On table be spread snow-white tablecloth; upon it be splendid porcelain service, and roast goose be steaming famously with its stuffing of apple and dry plum. And what be still more capital to behold be, goose hop down from dish, reel about on floor with knife and fork in its breast, till it come up to poor little girl; when - match go out and nothing but thick, cold, damp wall be leave behind. She light another match. Now there she be sitting under most magnificent Christmas tree: it be still larger, and more decorate than one which she have see through glass door in rich merchant's house.

Thousand of light be burning on green branch, and gaily-color picture, such as she have see in shop-window, look down upon her. Little maiden stretch out her hand toward them when… match go out. Light of Christmas tree rise higher and higher, she see them now as star in heaven; one fall down and form long trail of fire.

"Someone be just dead!" say little girl; for her old grandmother, only person who have love her, and who be now no more, have tell her, that when star fall, soul ascend to God.

She draw another match against wall: it be again light, and in luster there stand old grandmother, so bright and radiant, so mild, and with such expression of love.

"Grandmother!" cry little one. "Oh, take me with you! You go away when match burn out; you vanish like warm stove, like delicious roast goose, and like magnificent Christmas tree!" And she rub whole bundle of match quickly against wall, for she want to be quite sure of keeping her grandmother near her. And match give such brilliant light that it be brighter than at noon-day: never formerly have grandmother be so beautiful and so tall. She take little maiden, on her arm, and both fly in brightness and in joy so high, so very high, and then above be neither cold, nor hunger, nor anxiety - they be with God.

But in corner, at cold hour of dawn, sit poor girl, with rosy cheek and with smiling mouth, leaning against wall - freeze to death on last evening of old year. Stiff and stark sit child there with her match, of which one bundle have be burn. "She want to warm herself," people say. No one have slightest suspicion of what beautiful thing she have see; no one even dream of splendor in which, with her grandmother she have enter on joy of New Year.

VI. Sample B: The Little Match Girl (in original English)

The author had contacted with the Library of Congress for the copyrights status of "The Little Match Girl". The answer is that any work published before 1923 would be in the public domain because the copyright has long been expired. Any one would be free to use a public domain works without asking permission.

The author of "The Little Match Girl" was Hans Christian Andersen. He was born on April 2, 1805, died on August 4, 1875. So, his work can be found in the public domain with variety web sites as shown bellow.

http://www.cordula.ws/s-littlematchen.html

http://www.carols.org.uk/the_little_match_seller_hans_christian_anderson_snow.htm

http://classiclit.about.com/od/christmasstoriesholiday/a/aa_littlematch.htm

http://www.youtube.com/watch?v=pTt7ampNJL0

For the convenience to readers, the author feels it safe to quote it here as well starting on the next paragraph.

"The Little Match Girl"

Most terribly cold it was; it snowed, and was nearly quite dark, and evening - the last evening of the year. In this cold and darkness there went along the street a poor little girl, bareheaded, and with naked feet. When she left home she had slippers on, it is true; but what was the good of that? They were very large slippers, which her mother had hitherto worn; so large were they; and the poor little thing lost them as she scuffled away across the street, because of two carriages that rolled by dreadfully fast.

One slipper was nowhere to be found; the other had been laid hold of by an urchin, and off he ran with it; he thought it would do capitally for a cradle when he some day or other should have children himself. So the little maiden walked on with her tiny naked feet, that were quite red and blue from cold. She carried a quantity of matches in an old apron, and she held a bundle of them in her hand. Nobody had bought anything of her the whole livelong day; no one had given her a single farthing.

She crept along trembling with cold and hunger - a very picture of sorrow, the poor little thing!

The flakes of snow covered her long fair hair, which fell in beautiful curls around her neck; but of that, of course, she never once now thought. From all the windows the candles were gleaming, and it smelt so deliciously of roast goose, for you know it was New Year's Eve; yes, of that she thought.

In a corner formed by two houses, of which one advanced more than the other, she seated herself down and cowered together. Her little feet she had drawn close up to her, but she grew colder and colder, and to go home she did not venture, for she had not sold any matches and could not bring a farthing of money: from her father she would certainly get blows, and at home it was cold too, for above her she had only the roof, through which the wind whistled, even though the largest cracks were stopped up with straw and rags.

Her little hands were almost numbed with cold. Oh! a match might afford her a world of comfort, if she only dared take a single one out of the bundle, draw it against the wall, and warm her fingers by it. She drew one out. "Rischt!" how it blazed, how it burnt! It was a warm, bright flame, like a candle, as she held her hands over it: it was a wonderful light. It seemed really to the little maiden as though she were sitting before a large iron stove, with burnished brass feet and a brass ornament at top. The fire burned with such blessed influence; it warmed so delightfully. The little girl had already stretched out her feet to warm them too; but - the small flame went out, the stove vanished: she had only the remains of the burnt-out match in her hand.

She rubbed another against the wall: it burned brightly, and where the light fell on the wall, there the wall became transparent like a veil, so that she could see into the room. On the table was spread a snow-white tablecloth; upon it was a splendid porcelain service, and the roast goose was steaming famously with its stuffing of apple and dried plums. And what was still more capital to behold was, the goose hopped down from the dish, reeled about on the floor with knife and fork in its breast, till it came up to the poor little girl; when--the match went out and nothing but the thick, cold, damp wall was left behind. She lighted another match. Now there she was sitting under the most magnificent Christmas tree: it was still larger, and more decorated than the one which she had seen through the glass door in the rich merchant's house.

Thousands of lights were burning on the green branches, and gaily-colored pictures, such as she had seen in the shop-windows, looked down upon her. The little maiden stretched out her hands towards them when…the match went out. The lights of the Christmas tree rose higher and higher, she saw them now as stars in heaven; one fell down and formed a long trail of fire.

"Someone is just dead!" said the little girl; for her old grandmother, the only person who had loved her, and who was now no more, had told her, that when a star falls, a soul ascends to God.

She drew another match against the wall: it was again light, and in the luster there stood the old grandmother, so bright and radiant, so mild, and with such an expression of love.

"Grandmother!" cried the little one. "Oh, take me with you! You go away when the match burns out; you vanish like the warm stove, like the delicious roast goose, and like the magnificent Christmas tree!" And she rubbed the whole bundle of matches quickly against the wall, for she wanted to be quite sure of keeping her grandmother near her. And the matches gave such a brilliant light that it was brighter than at noon-day: never formerly had the grandmother been so beautiful and so tall. She took the little maiden, on her arm, and both flew in brightness and in joy so high, so very high, and then above was neither cold, nor hunger, nor anxiety - they were with God.

But in the corner, at the cold hour of dawn, sat the poor girl, with rosy cheeks and with a smiling mouth, leaning against the wall - frozen to death on the last evening of the old year. Stiff and stark sat the child there with her matches, of which one bundle had been burnt. "She wanted to warm herself," people said. No one had the slightest suspicion of what beautiful things she had seen; no one even dreamed of the splendor in which, with her grandmother she had entered on the joys of a new year.

VII. If the Queen wishes to learn from Emperor Qin?

Emperor Qin was also spelled as Chin Shih Huang (or, Chin Shih Huang Dih, that means in Chinese - The Starting King of all Kings of Chin dynasty); 259 BC – 210 BC. He was the king of the State of Qin from 246 BC to 221 BC, during the Warring States Period. He became the first emperor of a unified China in 221 BC. (The author learnt that the word China might be originally derived from the word "Chin" + "a".) He ruled until his death in 210 BC at the age of 49. He undertook gigantic projects, including the Great Wall of China, which shall be more correctly to be translated as the Long Castle, because of the original Chinese characters Chang Cheng real meaning (Chang = long; Cheng = castle for its defensive function). The rebuilt Ming walls measure 8,850 km, or, 5,500 mi. Chin Shih Huang also ordered to build the famous underground mausoleum guarded by 8,000 life-sized Terracotta soldiers, 130 chariots with 520 horses and 150 cavalry horses, and a massive national road system. Refer to a site at

http://en.wikipedia.org/wiki/Emperor_Qin

Besides, the Emperor Qin Shih Huang had made the order to unify the Chinese characters, which were written in different forms in other six states previously before China was centralized as one nation.

Now, the Queen of Britain, Elizabeth II, has a good chance to learn from Emperor Qin, not for his ruthless and crucial to treat his people, but one smart thing that he had used political power to unify the deviated written form of Chinese characters, which benefited the nation a lot. I feel that Elizabeth II shall be the most qualified person, who will have the authority to organize a committee, to transform the King's/Queen's English into a universal language for the entire world, per se,

Sapiensish what Johnson K. Gao sugested. Should her Majesty can follow my idea to reform English and build a solid Sapiensish, she will be greater.

From the point of view of history, it is the people, who are real heroes. However, a person's special position and individual force at certain period of time in the society could play a very important role. Suppose that Elizabeth II could invite the author of Sapiensish to explain the benefit of using Sapiensish, it could weight ten times more significant than that she had invited the Chinese young pianist Lang Lang to the Bukingham Place to perform piano. Unfortunately, she may not even be possible to receive this massage (although I had mail the file to her office few years ago before 2018) and invite me to explain to her about how to catch a great historical moment from which it can help her to seize an everlasting fame that the Emperor Qin had crowned in the human history. Sadly, there is no one around her who had the wisdom and courage to mention that point to her Majesty. I had tested if I can really reach her. My personal experience told me that such an invitation might be almost impossible, because I had mailed her Majesty three pieces of music CD, in which one CD is called as Gao's Music for Olympic Games, also an MTV of London Olympic Games' Theme Song composed by me to her office, long before the London Olympic Game's opening ceremony. But, to my deep sorrow, I got no any acknowledgment or thanks from her office. Refer to two sites bellow.

http://www.store.cdbaby.com/all/huanying

http://www.youtube.com/watch?v=4xLnvkof9iw&feature=plcp

Anyhow, for the benefit of mankind, I will try to mail a copy of this printed book to Her Majesty Queen once more. Alternatively, I will also sent out a gift copy of this Sapiensish to the President of the United States, or, an e-version to the Library of Congress, or, to the National Library of France. The later is my favorite, since I had sent a copy of my book "Prediction of Stock with Gao's Equation" to that library and I got a thanks letter from them very soon, which is a contrast to the gifts that I sent to the Queen of Britain. Of course, I will also mail a free copy of this version of Sapiensish to the Library of Congress, which gave me the feedback that to use "The Little Match Girl" in this pamphlet is safe.

Since the revision of the above file was encouraged by my recent article: "Outline of the World Leaders Education Institute", in which to develop a universal human language is one of goals of the institute, and to publish a book at lulu.com it requires a minimum page numbers, so, I would like to attach a copy of some related works of mine here, starting from this page.

VIII. Outline of the World Leaders Education Institute

Johnson K. Gao
January 28, 2018 in Dallas Texas

1. **Introduction**
The reliable philosophy is that everything shall have its beginning/creation/birth and its ending/extinction/death. From the evolutional point of view, the human being, Homo sapiens, was originated about 300,000 years ago. [1] According to the Johnson K. Gao's equation: E = $7B2^{44}$, the weight of human being's population could be heavier than the weight of the Earth in A. D. 3552 and the body of whole human being could cover the total land of the Earth in about 500~700 years calculated starting from A. D. 2012. [2, 3] So, if we consider the hazardous chemical pollution of the air, the radio waves generated by web sites, the sea level rising caused by global warming and radioactive nuclear wastes accumulated in environment, etc. the next few hundred of years will bring the human being to the critical point of existence. While the presidents/kings/queens currently lead their nations are not qualified to lead the future world, because of a simple reason that they are patriotism, and the patriotism only considers the national benefit higher than the whole mankind's benefit. Thus, we must educate future world leaders based on the Homo sapiensism, in order to prolong the human being's strategic longevity. The establishment of the World Leaders Education Institute is for that purpose.

2. **The aim of the World Leaders Education Institute**
The aim of the World Leaders Education Institute (WLEI) is to nurse and educate students to become the candidates of the future world wise leaders. They should learn and practice how to put the highest benefit of the whole human being in the privilege position. That means the mankind's benefit is higher than the individual nations' benefit. We must do the best for the elongation of human being's lifespan and to delay the doomsday to come.

3. **Headquarter and Divisions**
3.1. The Headquarter of the World Leaders Education Institute is temporary set on the web only with the reason that we are not sure which individual nation may compromise with the idea of promotion of the Homo sapiensism, which in some degree will against the nationalism.
3.2. For the financial reason, funding and banking and registration to the government and to have a physical space for operation of WLEI administration we need to establish some branches of World Leaders Education Institute and register it in some specific nations. Such that WLEI-America, WLEI-China, WLEI-Germany, WLEI-Japan, WLEI-south America, WLEI-India, WLEI-Russia, WLEI-Australia, WLEI-France, WLEI-Germany, WLEI-Singapore, etc.

4. **Staffs, Teachers and Students**
We hope that staffs, teachers and students will finally become atheists. But, we will not prohibit theists to become the staffs, teachers and students of the World Leaders Education Institute, because that theists are huge parts of human being and the Homo sapiensism is for whole human being's benefit that include both atheists and theists' benefits. It is hard to verify the existence of God. It is

also difficult to verify the none-existence of God. The dog, the cat, the monkey, the insect, the bacteria, etc. are less intelligent than human being and all animals do not believe in God. Strangely, the human being is self-recognized as the most intelligent "animal" among all living things, and there exist a large part of human being, who have religion and who created the image of God and believe in God. It might be a shame to those "Top intelligent" persons of human being, whose intelligence are inferior to the dog, the cat, the monkey, the insect, the bacteria, etc. We Homo sapiensists have to work hardly to persuade those theists to accept evolutionary theory. However, it needs time and patience. So, at this moment, we must accept theists to work and study with us, as long as they agree to put the highest benefit for the whole human being, instead of to improperly insist on localists' or nationalists' benefits, and to do things that are conflict with mankind's benefit. And we believe that none Homo sapiensists can also contribute their knowledge and energy to help us to nurse world leaders with the spirit of Homo sapiensism, that is quite similar to the situation that none astronauts can nurse or educate real astronauts, and none Olympic championship winners can coach or train some athletes to become Olympic medal winners.

5. Departments and Common Courses

The second and/or third languages, the leadership training and human history are common courses that every student must learn. The institute will not set many departments. But, the following 13 departments are unique to the institute, which are for students to select as an enhanced specialty in the third year.

5.1. Department of Universal language Development
5.2. Department for the promotion of International Standardization Units
5.3. Department of Philosophy and Human History
5.4. Department of Religion Analysis and Leadership Building
5.5. Department of Desert Farming
5.6. Department of Ocean Engineering
5.7. Department of New Energy development
5.8. Department of Space Defense
5.9. Department of Transgenic Research
5.10. Department of Birth Control and Eugenics
5.11. Department of Epidemic Diseases Control and Individual Aging
5.12. Department of Moon-kite Project. [4]
5.13. Department of Radio Wave and Hazardous Radioactive Componds Control

6. Terms and tuition

We consider that the current high education system must go through a revolution to fit the computer age. The current education duration is too long. The fact that many courses studied are un-necessary courses for the fulfillment a degree and the teaching method of "stuffing foods to feed the duck" might be similar to force students to "deadly read books", to accept unimportant knowledge and to exhaust brain cells. Some courses studied might not be used for whole life of the students but only for the purpose to meet the requirement of a degree. That is a waste of "the golden age" of student and to suppress young men's creativity at the most creative age of life, to prohibit them to do more meaningful and creative things. We will not ask students to become the worms of books. We will teach students the way of how to find the useful knowledge in time of need. That can save of time and tuition fee. The total study duration at WLEI will be shrunken to three years with six semesters. But, it shall be enough to complete a MS degree equivalent to other famous universities. The tuition fee of a fiscal year should be adjusted to around half of tuition fees of other moderate expensive colleges. And we will

increase the chances to visit high tech related laboratories, modernized manufacturing companies, go to foreign country to learn foreign language program, etc.
The six semesters are temporary planed as:
6.1. The life science semester (courses may include human anatomy, microbiology, neuroscience, Darwinism and evolution, health, nutrition and anti-aging, etc.);
6.2. Language and logic training semester (courses may include a second language of students' choice, such that English, Chinese, German, French, Russian, Japanese, Arabic, etc., which must be studies in the countries where that language is used. It needs no less than five months study abroad. The students must keep a mind to criticize the second language and absorb the good things in that a language in order to build a universal language that the WLEI is intend to develop. The logic training needs to select good textbooks.
6.3. Music and arts semester. We need to develop a multi-talented man. Music is an international language. It can express emotion without words. Before we can create a global common speaking language, students need at least listen to certain amount of famous music pieces, say 200 pieces of music, both happy and sorrow melodies, from different nations, and learn to play one instrument. Also students need to learn western and oriental style painting basic techniques, chess playing and fight training, music composition and video production, etc.
6.4. Chemistry and Physics semester. (courses may include Inorganic Chemistry, Organic Chemistry, General Physics and Quantum Physics. Visiting aerospace lab, plastic manufactory plant, wind hole, nuclear reaction facilities, ocean oil drilling well platform, solar energy and wind energy equipment manufacturing companies, desert farming industry, etc.).
6.5. Speech and leadership training. Internship in Capital Hill or other government administration organizations, or, in other counties, or, in the United Nations. Another alteration is to serve for certain period of time to Al Gore's Climate reality organization. That will in combination with semester 6.6.
6.6. Special thesis semester. Select one of above listed Departments and write a thesis that shall be meaningful to solve the currently international conflict, such as how to settle certain territory conflict that will benefit to the whole human being instead for the benefit to X-nation. The thesis must also go through defense procedure and talk on the GGG forum, and the best thesis should be awarded with annual GGG prize.

7. Degrees and Thesis

The degree is equivalent to master degree through three years study. The graduates must presented to the GGG Forum with any topics such that the point of view to solve an international problem or why and how to dissolve the conflict among different nations, or scientific prediction of some difficult problems.

8. Graduation Ceremony

Graduation ceremony is a necessary to increase students' enthusiasm and responsibility to serve the society. The institute will not ask graduates to wear academic gong and hat for graduation ceremony. Wearing old-fashioned academic gown, which seems not to be conformed to the modern spirit. Instead, the female students could choose to wear Hawaiian flower wreaths and leave-aprons. The male students could apply the face-painting similar to New Zealand tribe's tattoo style or the Beijing Opera face-painting and wearing Batsman's cloaks, with the meaning to bring back human natural beauty and heroic expression to increase the warmer cerebration air.

9. Institutional Song

Before a finalized Institutional Song is selected, temporary we may use the song below.

世界領袖教育學院院歌

高魁雄詞曲

2018 年 1 月

萬物有生必有亡。
世界末日遲早會臨降。
大自然並未為恐龍的滅絕而哭泣;

大自然也不會為人類末日而悲傷。
求神拜佛不靈;
人類自救才存希望。
讓我們奮起,
為了實現智人主義而奔忙。
願智人義放光芒。

世界领袖教育学院院歌(简体)
高魁雄词曲
2018 年 1 月

万物有生必有亡。
世界末日迟早会临降。
大自然并未为恐龙的灭绝而哭泣;
大自然也不会为人类末日而悲伤。
求神拜佛不灵;
人类自救才存希望。
让我们奋起,
为了实现智人主义而奔忙。
愿智人义放光芒。

(English translation)
Song of the World Leaders Education Institute
Johnson K. Gao
January 2018

All things have their birth as well as their death.
The Doomsday of the world will fall sooner or later.
The Nature did not cry for the extinction of dinosaurs;
The Nature will not express sorrow for the end of mankind.

Pray to the God and worship Buddha are useless;
Human's self-saver is the only hope.
Let us awake and arise -
Struggling for the realization of Homo sapiensism.
May the Homo sapiensism shine.

註釋:

第一句是指一種唯物主義的哲學思想。那大概是人類必須服從的世界觀。
第二句中的"臨降"二字是為了押韻而倒裝。
第三句, 第四句是擬人法, 將"大自然"比作人的形象。
第五句, 第六句是反對神創論和迷信, 提倡人類自救。
最后一句, "為了實現智人主義"是全曲的核心。"奔忙"二字意為因末日太近了, 走路不行, 得奔跑。要去除地方主義和愛國主義, 為了實現智人主義而忙碌。

Note:

The first sentence refers to a kind of materialist philosophical thinking. That kind of world point of view is probably the human being must obey.
In the second sentence, the words "coming and down" are flipped for rhyming.
The third sentence and the fourth sentence are anthropomorphic law, which refer to the "nature" as a human image.
The fifth sentence and the sixth sentence are against the God creationism and superstition and to promote human self-help.
The last sentence, "for the realization of Homo sapiensism" is the core of the whole song. The word "running" means the that the doomsday well come very fast and we should be fast to avoid its too late, and we should work diligently, to remove the localism and patriotism, in order to achieve Homo sapiensism.

10. Institutional Medal

WWWW mean We Work for Whole World.

11. Fund raising

Each sub-WLEI, such that WLEI-America, shall find the way to get its financial support by fund raising in the country that permit the registration of the sub-WLEI and lawfully to establish the GGG fund. And the sub-WLEI must donate a certain percentage of money collected to headquarter for organizing the worldwide events.

12. GGG (Gore-Gao-Globalization) Forum

The name of the GGG forum is temporary set up. That is because Al Gore is the Nobel Prize winner and the first person to organize the Climate Reality to promote world environmental protection.

Johnson K. Gao is the first person to propose the idea of Homo sapiesism and he published a book entitled as E = 7B2^44 Gao's Equation in relation to three tides of global immigration and strategic longevity. [2,3]

12.1. GGG Forum Membership personal number

There is a human population about 7 billion people in the world. To issue a personal membership of GGG forum we use the following method.

The first three letters mean member's family name, given name and gender.

Like GJM = Johnson Gao, male

Followed by eight Arabic number for birthday

Like 19370503 = May third, 1937.

Followed by two letters of the initial of current residency (or citizenship).

Like US = United States.

Because there are 26 letters for family name, 26 letters for given name and 2 for male or female. If one out of 100 people could be interested in the GGG forum (that percentage is too happy than we expected), 365 for the possibility of one day out of one year for a unique birth days and there are 195 nations in the world.
Then, the chance of repeating might be approximately to
7,000,000,000 divided by (26 x 26 x 2 x 100 x 365 x 195)
Or,
$7 \times 10^{9}/9622860000 = 0.72743446335$
Which is less than 1.
That means
GJM19370503US is a unique person among 7 billion of population.
If there could appear any repeating, we can add a number selected from 01~99 to the end, such that it will turns to GJM19370503US-01.
The postfix -01 can be omitted in most of the case, suppose that no other member will cause confusion.
Based on that membership number, other people can get the information that that member has the family name starting with the letter G, and given name starting with the letter J; It is a male, M, and age of 81 (counted in A. D. 2018 – 1937 = 81) and he lives in the United States of America.
12.2. Although people can use that rule to write out the membership number by themselves, to let it officially active, application is needed. To apply for a membership number, please e-mail your family name, given name, gender, home address, email address, and education and skills to jkxgao@gmail.com

13. GGG prize and GGG Fund

The GGG prize is not like the Nobel Prize [6] with huge amount of money awarded to the prizewinner. The amount of money of GGG prize is very small, at least in the beginning, because the starting of the GGG fund could be only $1.00 donated by J. K. Gao, and promised by two other persons with $2.00 (Many US companies start to run their business with the seeds money of One dollar bill). If the prize is 5% of the GGG fund, the bottom line of GGG Prize winner may only to receive 15 cent. But, its meaning could be far more than the Nobel Prize, since it is aimed to award to prizewinners, who could have contributed great ideal to prolong the whole mankind's strategic longevity and to delay the Doomsday to come. That is just like what Alfred Nobel wrote: **"For the greatest benefit to mankind."** (It said in March 17, 2017 J. K. Gao to Nobel Forum organization e-mail: *"I believe that should Nobel be alive now and read my equation E = 7B2^44, with which the Doomsday of human being can be calculated and that the human being's strategic longevity could be adjusted by doubling time (years) of human population needed, he might be excited and want to award Johnson K. Gao a special Nobel prize."*)
" So, the GGG prizewinners must be considered to get highest honor compatible to all of those Nobel Prize winners. The amount of money of GGG prize will be increased in the future, when the GGG fund grows bigger. A proposal written by J. K. Gao few days ago indicated that it may needs to set the aim to raise a fund of $12,000,000 for the GGG to establish the WLEI. Among that amount of money $4,000,000 could be used for GGG forum. If the GGG prize is 5% of $4,000,000, each GGG prizewinner could receive $200,000.
I am 80 years of age now and my two eyes had got 5 surgeries. Even my intimate family members are laughing at me and said: " You are day dreaming". But, nowadays dreaming is popular among big leaders, such that China Dreaming. For the historical reason, I am very poor.

That is why I could only donate $1.00 to the GGG fund at this moment. However, recently I published an article at Journal of Eye Diseases and Disorders [7] on A Nutritional Eye Washing Solution (NEWS) Concentrated that Could Improve the Sharpness of Vision. In case that the method could be patented/commercialized, and could be profitable, I will donate more money to GGG fund. You guys may look down upon me that I am learning from Mr. Wu Xun, a beggar, who saved a lot of hard-earned money in order to establish a free school. [8] If it is not my proposal to establish a GGG forum, sooner or later someone will be raised. In view of the urgent need to delay the onset of the doomsday, it is better that I made it earlier.

14. Vice Presidents and Staffs needed

We need to recruit vice presidents and staffs for WLEI-America. Before we can reach the aim of fundraising of $12,000,000, we can only accept those people who can offer part time work on the volunteer base, which shall have the historical honor with a special certification. Several vice president positions of the WLEI are now open. Staffs of various skills with or without Ph. D. or MS degree are also needed. The aimed salary in the future is within a range of $60,000~120,000 per year, when the funding is available.

15. Call on papers

The GGG forum is open to every one, at least 18 years of age or older, male or female of any nationality, to submit any topics with the importance to improve human being's healthy and comfortable living on the Earth and/or to increase the whole human being's longevity and/or to resolve conflicts between multi-nations and/or any proposals that may bring the great benefit to the Homo sapiens. Article must have an abstract in English of 300-500 words. The text shall be no more than 10,000 words and it must be written in English, or, Chinese, or, French, or, Russian. Other languages are temporary not accepted. Alternatively, video presentation in English or Chinese is accepted also. For the year 2018 two subjects, one on "How to develop a universal world language" and another on "Discussion or suggestion on refugees problem in Germany and European nations" are most welcome. Author must be a single person with mailing address and e-mail contact, but not a group of persons. Please e-mail file to jkxgao@gmail.com.

Literature cited

1. http://www.newsweek.com/human-evolution-homo-sapiens-earliest-fossils-morocco-622544
2. http://www.lulu.com/shop/johnson-k-gao/e-7b244-gaos-equation-in-relation-to-three-tides-of-global-immigration-and-strategic-longevity/paperback/product-23111539.html?ppn=1
3. https://www.amazon.com/Equation-relation-immigration-strategic-longevity/dp/1365772098
4. Moon-kite project is a hypothetical science fiction engineering project, which intend to build a long cable to connect the Earth and the moon, that may generate huge amount of electricity and carry many super sonic transportation vehicles due to Earth rotation and the lunar orbital rotations.
5. https://www.climaterealityproject.org
6. https://www.nobelprize.org
7. https://www.omicsonline.org/open-access/A-Nutritional-Eye-Washing-Solution-News-Concentrated-that-could-Improve-the-sharpness-of-vision.pdf
https://www.youtube.com/watch?v=ZsviQDxTjdY

Three Attachments

Four people's feedbacks are copied as follows.

Jan. 18, 2018
Mr. F Feedback
Great idea. Congrats. 100% support for sure.

This world needs to be educated, from top to bottom and vice versa.

Jan. 18, 2018
Mr. Z feedback
非常赞同!

爱国主义 is a thing of the past. Today we face more challenges of human survival as a whole than of one nation over another. 在一个融通的世界里，每一个人每一个民族都是世界公民、属于"地球村"的，特别是在这个互联网时代 — 互联网已经把我们紧紧地拉在一起了。在这环境中，民族主义岂不等同于种族主义? ! 民族主义跟种族主义相比，难道能说前者比后者更好吗? 一个是以民族（实际上是演变的地理界限）为区分，一个是以皮肤颜色为区分。这两在当今的互联网时代、在这大"地球村"里都是扯蛋!

So, instead, we should be talking about humanism, not patriotism, which is the equivalent of racism.

其实在圣经里上帝早就给了我们启示 — 耶稣基督的救恩岂是只给以色列民族吗? 不是! 是给我们全人类的，不仅犹太人 (jews) 还有外邦人(gentiles)。

Yes, it is time, it is HIGH time, that we have a true leader to have a vision of the whole world, of all the nations, to take on the challenges of the new age — the age of the CONNECTED WORLD, the age of the EARTH VILLAGE.

Best regards,
Ray

Jan. 27, 2018
Mr. L feedback
高先生您好！ 思想超前活跃！ 创作热情不减当年！
这首院歌规模浩大，气势磅礴!
歌词短小精干，一目了然，没有引经据典，没有造揉做作，没有空洞的口号，一看二唱，大家一切都会明白!

曲调更是调动了一切作曲技艺，以臻完美！ 尤其可贵的是，使用 A 调，使低音更抒情婉约，高音益发嘹亮高亢！ 还有一点作者处理得非常巧妙，歌曲开头用小调，和歌词的情绪一样，頗为忧虑；到结束时，也和歌词的精神相吻合，用大调来作结，显得格外激昂奔放！ 足見作曲者用心良苦，看到作曲水平立見高下！
盼望有更多作品问世！ 不当之处，请賜教！
楼

发自我的 iPad

Jan. 20, 2018
Mr. Y feedback
高先生 韦老师：
你们好！ 我们敬佩高先生的精神！ 真是多才多艺！
祝福你们健康快乐幸福！
乐平

发自我的 iPad

March 2, 2917
From Prof. C:
Dear Prof. 高魁雄:

You are right. You will be certainly greater than 爱因斯坦 if you can use your equation to predict the time of 世界末日.

IX. The Ultimate Longevity of Mankind

Johnson K. Gao
Research Professor in Cell Biology retired from the University of Cincinnati College of Medicine, Cincinnati, OH
Current address: 5609 Harbor Town Drive, Garland, TX 75044, USA
E-mail: jkxgao@gmail.com
December 23, 2017

Abstract

It is a weird phenomenon that the ability of reproduction of human being, with which the human being could exist and prolong, could potentially become the ultimate killer of mankind. If the present population doubling time could not be properly controlled, the "reproduction" will go to the opposite, "perishing" or "extinction". Gao's equation: $E = 7B2^{44}$ would lead the weight of entire human population equal to the weight of the Earth. The multiplication of population will lead to the doomsday around the A. D. 3552 or earlier. The time needed to cover all the surface of the Earth with human bodies will be much earlier than A. D. 3552. Samples of people occupying the limited lands had appeared in many real life situations like pilgrims in Mecca. That is the prelude of the condition of doomsday of the world. The ultimate longevity of whole human being could not simply base on individuals' tactics of personal health and longevity. But, It needs to promote Homo sapiensism, which considers the highest benefit of whole mankind instead of single nation's benefit. It is a higher level than patriotism. Unfortunately, almost no any current presidents, or, kings/queens of various countries, who stopped at patriotism stage, can be qualified to lead the world. So, it is an urgent project to establish a World Leaders Education Institute to nurse future global leaders to prolong the longevity of whole human being and reduce the speed towards doomsday.

An old friend of mine and alumnus of the Nanjing University, also a colleague of the Chinese Academy of Sciences, who was also as a lifeguard together with me of the swimming pool, which belongs the Chinese Academy of Sciences in Shanghai; More importantly, he is one of authorities in the computational macromolecular structure in the world, professor Zhou Guo-cheng (English name Kuo-Chen Chou) recently sent me his new article - "An unprecedented revolution in medicinal chemistry driven by advances in biological science". That article was published in the Journal of Medicinal Chemistry, 2017, No. 17, pp. 2337-2358. It is a review article, containing 21 pages and 577 references cited. The first sentence of that article writes: "The eternal or ultimate goal of medicinal chemistry is to find the most effective way to treat various diseases and to extend human being's life as long as possible." My current article is to discuss with Dr. K. C. Chou.

As the ancient Chinese saying goes: "英雄所見略同" (Different heroes may have the same vision). "The eternal or ultimate goal of medicinal chemistry is to find the most effective way to treat (and prevent) all kinds of diseases and to extend the life of human being (although death is inevitable). (words in parenthesis were added by J. K. Gao for more accuracy). Those words are similar to J. K. Gao's short video - "On the longevity of whole human being (Eng.V2) ". [1] However, the levels of consideration were quite different as it appears in one chapter of my book that I published at lulu.com. [2]

What I want to emphasize here is the weird phenomenon that the ability of reproduction of human being, with which the human being could exist and prolong, could potentially turn into the ultimate killer of entire mankind. That will lead to the doomsday around the A. D. 3552 or much earlier. If the present population doubling time could not be properly controlled, the "reproduction" will go to its opposite, "perishing" or "extinction." That's not cheating or teasing. I believe that my equation: $E = 7B2^{44}$, which is a sister equation of Einstein's equation $E = MC^2$, is true and reliable. I would like to tell you once again that the end of the world would come much earlier than A. D. 3552, because in that year, the weight of entire human population will equal to the weight of the Earth. The year needed to cover the land of the Earth with human bodies should be far earlier than A. D. 3552. For you to understand better, I want to quote my analysis from my book: (Printed in Italic)

Although there might exist a threatening from the out space super intelligent life forms, it seems to me the real potential threatening is more likely coming from the Earth, especially from the human activities directly. Among them the global pollution and the speed of world population increasing at an exponential rate are two major issues for special concern. Now, the world population had reached 7 billion in March 2012. I heard that the rate of doubling of human population is about 35 years. Shall we curiously ask a question: How many years later the weight of total mankind will equal to the weight of the whole Earth? The Earth has a weight of about 6×10^{24} *kg. The world population is about* 7×10^{9}*. If the averaging weight per man is 50 kg, the total weight of human being is approximately about* 3.5×10^{11} *kg. The result of the double increment of* 2^{44} *obtained is* 17.59×10^{12}*. Now, let us use* 3.5×10^{11} *kg multiply by* 17.59×10^{12}*. It produces* 6.15×10^{24} *kg, which is a little heavier than the weight of the Earth. For easy to remember, here is a short equation of mine:*

$$\boldsymbol{E = 7B2^{44}}$$

*Where **E** denotes the equivalent weight to the Earth. **B** denotes the total weight of one billion of human population, suppose that the average body weight is 50 kg/man. I hope that the equation might become a sister equation to the famous Albert Einstein's equation, because of their rather similar appearances, although where **E** has different meaning...*

However, as I had pointed out that human beings are not aquatic animals, but rather terrestrial organisms. The time to cover all the surface of Earth with human bodies will be much earlier than A. D. 3552. Samples of people occupying the limited lands had appeared in many real life situations. They are the prelude of the condition of doomsday of the world, such as photographic images of pilgrims in Mecca; [3-5] Tourists gathered in the Great Wall; [6] US presidential rally and Venezuelan rally. [7. 8]

The idea for seeking the extension of the life of the whole human being is quite different from the idea for seeking personal longevity. Professor Chou said: "The eternal or ultimate goal of medicinal chemistry is to find the most effective way to treat various diseases and to extend human life as much as possible." To me, that belongs to the category of personal tactical longevity. My calculation of the last days or how to prolong the life of the entire human being - which can be done by adjusting the time needed to multiply the population, belongs to the strategic longevity of whole mankind. In the modern world, family planning, war, industrial pollution, greenhouse effect and sea-level rising, serious epidemics and even the advanced medical treatment, that can save more lives are all factors and that can change the population growth, or, that can slow down the rate at which mankind can reach the end of the world, are related to the strategic longevity of whole human being.

Whether you agree with my opinion or not, I predict that three waves of major immigration will inevitably occur around the world. The first wave of global migration is the wave of immigrants from poor or underdeveloped countries seeking their wealth and wellbeing towards rich and well-developed countries. The recent refugee issue is a prelude to this wave of immigration, in which the population in poor and underdeveloped countries has moved to the higher living standard countries. [9-12] Remember, an average of about 982.28 square meters of arable land per person is a threshold, which determines the direction of immigration. China is now under that threshold, which has an average of about 781.2 square meters. Chinese people will intend to seek immigration out of China. That is quite obvious. US is now much higher than that threshold, which has an average of 5,062.4 square meters per person. Naturally, Chinese move to US is a reasonable choice.

The second wave of global migration is the shift of the population from fertile arable land to exposed mountains and deserts, which has resulted in less and less living space in fertile agricultural lands due to population growth.[13-16] Another quote from my book: (Printed in Italic)

If the calculation is based on the entire Earth-land surface and the average area required by a man:
Because $E_S = m7B_S\, 2^X$
So, that $148.3 \times 10^{12}\, M^2 = 982.28\, M^2 \times 7 \times 10^9 \times 2^X$
Or, 2^X *equals to* $148.3 \times 10^{12}\, M^2$ *to be divided by* $982.28\, M^2 \times 7 \times 10^9$
Or, $2^X = 21.568$
When $X = 4$, $2^4 = 16$, *which is less than 21.568.*
When $X = 5$, $2^5 = 32$, *which is greater than 21.568.*
When $X = 4.44$ *when,* $2^{4.44} = 21.706$, *the value has more than 21.568.*
If the world population doubling time is 35 years, then 35 years x 4.44 = 155.4 years.
If the world population doubling time is 50 years, then 50 years x 4.44 = 222 years.
Since in the year A. D. 2012, the entire world's population had reached seven billion. We used the year A. D. 2012 + 155.4 = A. D. 2167.4; we use the year A. D. 2012 + 222 = A. D. 2234.
So, the continuation from A. D. 2107 ~ 2147 extending to A. D. 2167.4 ~ 2234 and between that duration, the more people give birth, the less life land could be shared with. People's lives will change from a well being status to a global poverty. It will appear the world's second immigration climax. The characteristic of that second climax of immigration is its direction towards barren mountains and vast deserts.

The third wave of global immigration is crowded human migration from the mainland to the vast oceans. This process has begun in some small part of the globe. This is the window of the future. [17, 18]

Don't think that my equation is useless. The industrial development must obey to or cooperate with this global wave of immigrants. It is the need of the people, something that no one can stop it by building the "New Great Wall." As the Chinese saying goes:

"道高一尺，魔高一丈。" (When the saints raise one foot high; The devils pop-up three yards higher). As long as mankind remains to double its population in a certain period of time, the immigration tides cannot be stopped. That is an irresistible demand. Even on the case of the young generation to select major for attending university, they have to consider my equation, such that the oceanology and desert farming could become hot few hundred years later. A detailed calculation of the immigration schedule can be found in my book [2] and in my videos. [19, 20] The video [19] has most accurate calculation for the exact year of three different immigration tides to come. Readers are highly encouraged to watch that video.

Put all in a nutshell, the human strategic longevity is largely determined by political forces. It can hardly be determined by any drugs. Therefore, in order to extend the life expectancy of the Homo sapiens, we must advocate Homo Sapiensism (humanism) than patriotism. If all humanity must die, no one, no countries can survive. My equation $E = 7B2^{44}$ will determine the final human life expectancy. That is what I want to require people when they remember Prof. Chou's words - "The eternal or ultimate goal of medicinal chemistry is to find the most effective way to treat (and prevent) all kinds of diseases and to extend the life of human being (even though death is inevitable - words in parenthesis were added by J. K. Gao)." The ultimate of whole human being's longevity could not be simply based on individuals' tactics of personal health and longevity. On the contrary, it needs to promote Homo Sapiensism, which is a higher level than patriotism in human being social development. Unfortunately, at this moment, almost no any ongoing presidents or kings/Queens of various countries are still stopped only at patriotism stage. They are not qualified to lead the future world, because patriotism limited their thinking and their abilities and their leadership. So, it is an urgent projcct to establish a World Leader Education Institute to nurse future global leaders in order to prolong the longevity of whole human being. People may laugh at me that a none-Nobel Prize Winner and none president wants to teach Nobel Prize winners and presidents. However, the history may convince you all that my prediction is right. Thanks. I would like to quote my own words in my published book [2] to finish this article.
"Originally, there were no any roads under the heaven, on the Earth. More people to walk through, the road forms by itself, naturally." - Johnson Gao translated from Chinese words by Loo Shyun (Lu Xun).

"Failure is the mother, who gave birth to the son with the name called Success." - Johnson Gao translated from a Chinese old saying.

"The mountain pass will appear to the view only when your wagon has reached the foot of a hill." "When a boat is approaching to the arch of a bridge, it will turn straight by itself." - Johnson Gao translated from a Chinese old saying.

Literature

1. https://www.youtube.com/watch?v=B7x1OmOVp0w
2. Johnson K. Gao edited book "E = 7B2[44], Gao's equation in relation to three global immigration and strategic longevity" (ISBN 9781365772092) http://www.lulu.com/shop/johnson-k-gao/e-7b244-gaos-equation-in-relation-to-three-tides-of-global-immigration-and-strategic-longevity/paperback/product-23111539.html
3. https://specialtopicsinreligionuno.files.wordpress.com/2015/04/kaaba.jpg
4. https://www.nmisr.com/wp-content/uploads/2017/06/mcraim-_74_.jpg
5. https://aftabahmadkhokar.files.wordpress.com/2014/10/10698538_778846575510557_562213609083965891_n.jpg
6. https://web.stanford.edu/group/ccr/blog/crowded-great-wall-01.jpg
7. http://media.zenfs.com/en_us/News/Reuters/2012-10-04T213124Z_882009714_GM1E8A50F0D01_RTRMADP_3_USA-CAMPAIGN.JPG
8. http://fiscaltoday.com/images/2013/04/opposition-candidate-draws-gigantic-crowd-in-venezuelan-election-rally_wuozn_1.jpg
9. http://www.anu.edu.au/files/styles/anu_full_920_518/public/event_submission/city2surf-crowd-people-australia-aap.jpg?itok=aOPzrmYr
10. http://spiritualsidekick.com/wp-content/uploads/2012/09/crowd.jpg
11. http://www.hindustantimes.com/rf/image_size_800x600/HT/p1/2011/12/11/Incoming/Pictures/780989_Wallpaper2.jpg
12. http://s.newsweek.com/sites/www.newsweek.com/files/2015/09/18/0918croatia-refugees-migrants.jpg
13. http://static5.businessinsider.com/image/5220e1f969bedde8218b456a/this-is-what-it-looks-like-when-68000-people-build-a-temporary-city-in-the-nevada-desert.jpg
14. http://i.dailymail.co.uk/i/pix/2014/08/28/1409234340964_wps_41_quatar_Boulevard_and_Plaz.jpg
15. https://i.redditmedia.com/te7cR0Shmr4WPNhSoNOx8zicP5ttRIYTSbflyNX3Ai4.jpg?w=1024&s=99fdefeb7b6b5d0ce12f95e13e8b5c45
16. http://assets.inhabitat.com/wp-content/blogs.dir/1/files/2017/04/Freedomes-SunCity-Camp-Mars-889x592.jpg
17. https://www.designboom.com/wp-content/uploads/2013/10/phil-pauley-sub-biosphere-2-designboom-01.jpg
18. https://cdn6.psdstr.com/wp-content/uploads/2013/5/23/maritime-city-psd.jpg
19. https://www.youtube.com/watch?v=RwFsSWqZS74&t=927s
20. https://www.youtube.com/watch?v=jKbIfrai6xk&t=2758s

X. People who live in those countries with less arable land per person have to seek immigration to countries with more arable land per person

https://en.wikipedia.org/wiki/Land_use_statistics_by_country

https://en.wikipedia.org/wiki/List_of_countries_and_dependencies_by_population

Use arable land of a specific country or region (such that Taiwan) divided by the population of that country or region, you will get the figure of square meters of the arable land per person among all the residents live in those areas. The followings are 12 samples that I had selected and calculated out by using the above two sites.

1. Taiwan 6,084,000,000 M^2 / 23,566,853 = 258.2 M^2
2. Japan 44,226,000,000 M^2 / 126,700,000 = 349.1 M^2
3. Swaziland 4,213,000,000 M^2 / 8,465,234 = 497.7 M^2
4. China 1,084,462,000,000 M^2 / 1,388,250,000 = 781.2 M^2
5. Italy 68,697,000,000 M^2 / 60,501,718 = 1,135.5 M^2
6. India 1,753,694,000,000 M^2 / 1,325,630,000 = 1,322.9 M^2
7. Germany 121,737,000,000 M^2 / 82800000 = 1,470.3 M^2
8. Mexico 231,799,000,000 M^2 /123,675,351 = 1,874.3 M^2
9. Brazil 732,359,000,000 M^2 / 208,433,000 = 4,986.5 M^2
10. USA 1,652,028,000,000 M^2 / 326,332,000 = 5,062.4 M^2
11. Russia 1,248,169,000,000 M^2 / 146,867,905 = 8,498.6 M^2
12. Canada 469,281,000,000 M^2 / 36,966,900 = 12,694.6 M^2

From No. 1 to No. 12, the average arable land square meters per person are from less to more. Here is what I quoted from my book to you, that 982.28 square meters of arable land/person are the minimum for sustaining a comfortable life. (Page 26~27 of the site below, printed in Italic)

http://www.lulu.com/shop/johnson-k-gao/product-23111539.html
(or search ISBN 9781365772092)

Es = m7Bs 2^X
Although the total area of the Earth is Es = 148,300,000 kM^2, the Earth's land surface comprises arable land, mountain, desert, none soil covered rocks. The arable land of the Earth (agricultural farm land Ef) is only about 44,682,307 square kilometers, or, 4.4682×10^{13} square meters.
First, let us consider only the agricultural land (Ef).
Because Ef = m7Bs 2^X, so that 4.4682×10^{13} M^2 = $982.28 \times 7 \times 10^9 \times 2^X$
Then 2^X equals to that 4.4682×10^{13} M^2 is divided by 982.28 $M^2 \times 7 \times 10^9 \times 2^X$ that equal to 6.498. It is less than 6.5.
When X = 2, then, $2^2 = 4$, the value is less than 6.498.
When X = 3, then, $2^3 = 8$, which is greater than 6.498.
When X = 2.7, then, $2^{2.7} = 6.498$, the value is just the same as 6.498.
If the world population doubling time is 35 years, then, 35 years x 2.7 = 94.5 years.
If the world population doubling time is 50 years, then, 50 year x 2.7 = 135 years. In the year A. D. 2012, the entire world's population had reached seven billion. We use A. D. 2012 + 95 = A. D. 2107; we use the year A. D. 2012 + 135 = A. D. 2147.

Starting from A. D. 2012 until around the years A. D. 2107 ~ 2147 (nearly a century), there will appear the first immigrant climax. The characteristics of that climax of immigration will express that the immigrants from those countries, with the situation that the population density is relatively high, but the economic level is relatively low, such as India, China, African nations, the Middle East regions to those countries, with the situation that the economic development is faster and the that the living standard is more affluent, such as the United States, Germany, Canada, Australia and other European nations. This is for the purpose of eliminating poverty, improving the condition of living, or even getting rich faster. Due to the fact that the modern transportation tools have been developed so well, such that trains, ships, aircraft, etc., it is very convenient to shift the population from one region to another region, which makes it possible either to do the single cases of legal immigration, or, herds of illegal remote population migration, not only because there exist such kind of needs, but also it becomes relatively easy to achieve. The currently influx of millions of refugees might be considered as a prelude to that first tide of immigration.

Today is the Christmas of 2017 that I am writing this article. That means five years have passed since 2012. The first immigration tide will soon begin the sixth year.

You can see from the above 12 samples. Taiwan, Japan, Swaziland and China are four areas where the average man can only get less 982.28 square meters of arable land/person. So, people live in those areas will have the tendency to pursue immigration to other countries, such that move to Canada (12,694.6 M^2/person), USA (5,062.4 M^2/person), Russia (8,498.6 M^2/person) and Brazil (4,986.5 M^2/person).

Although Italy, India, Germany and Mexico are four countries, people live there now can have more than 982.28 square meters of arable land/person, after 35 years or 50 years, they will double their population and get less than 982.28 square meters of arable land/person. That means around A. D. 2047 to 2062, Italian, Indian, German and Mexican people will seek immigration more urgently than now (A. D. 2018). We may ask where people in sample 1~8 will go? Of course they will select the sample 9~12 of above countries. The government of Germany has now accepted many refugees. But, the German people will find that might be a wrong policy. Because after one or two generations, German people will seek immigration out of Germany, don't mention to accept refugees or immigrants. Chinese people move to USA from 1980s to 2017 increased rapidly.

https://www.migrationpolicy.org/article/chinese-immigrants-united-states

The Chinese people came to USA in the year 2016 are 2,335,000. That figure will increase furthermore either legally or illegally.

Brazil, USA, Russia and Canada are like sponge that can absorb immigration from my calculation of the average that 982.28 square meters of arable land/person is a threshold. By which year two other immigration tides to come are described in my book at:

http://www.lulu.com/shop/johnson-k-gao/product-23111539.html
(or search ISBN 9781365772092)
Merry Christmas and a Happy New Year! (2018)

Johnson Gao, Ph D

Postscript

About 18 years ago, our family drove a trip to Florida. On the way back to Dallas Texas, my son Raymond F. Gao discussed with me in the car about how to develop a kind of universal language. And after I back home, I wrote the first version of "Singlish", which was a simplified English, and posted it on inter net, yahoo.com group, in October 2001.

I know Chinese (both Mandarin and Shanghai dialect) and English. I had also learnt Russian at high school. I studied German as a second foreign language through my Ph. D. course. Besides, I also self studied a little bit of Japanese and French. Raymond can speak more languages fluently than me. He knows Mandarin, Shanghai dialect, English, German, French, Spanish plus Polish. Based on those experiences, we can at least make some judgments on selection of which language could be more potential to be developed in to a universal language. Personally, I feel French sounds most beautiful like music. However, its pronunciation omitted many consonants in written form. Chinese characters are hieroglyphs, which belong to the top concise language and Chinese poems could be the number one in express deep feeling with less words and rhythmic charm. But, mandarin does not exist consonants with vocal cord vibration and Chinese characters are very difficult to remember or to write. Japanese is a hybridized language with hieroglyphs (Chinese characters) and semi-alphabetic-letter spelling, though the letter shapes are different from Latin alphabetic letters. And Japanese has no consonant-ended-vowels, so it is lack of poetic beauty and Japanese always put verbs to the end of sentence. The German language sounds to me to harsh to ears; The Russian language is an organic language. It has six grammatical formats or transformations for verbs and nouns. That is too complicate. And its letter-shape and pronunciation are not as sharp and pleasant hearing than English. Thus, personally I select English as a base or frame for the development of a universal language.

Later, I found that "Singlish" could cause confusion with Singapore local English, which was also called as "Singlish". The second version was modified and posted on scribd.com, in January 2005. From 1/1/2007 to 8/15/2012 that site has been visited 28,076 times. The highest peak of the daily counts were 847 on 5/23/2009. The third version was modified on August 14, 2012 and self-published. Unfortunately, very few people want to purchase that printed book. The forth-revised version was modified on February 2, 2015. This is the fifth version, and I called it as "Homo Sapiensish, or, Sapiensish". I hope the wave will turn to up direction again.

I shall not be 孤芳自赏 (smelling a single piece of the fragrant flower with self-appreciation only). I hope to find a group of talented people to make common contribution to develop a solid, easy to learn and logically reliable human common language – a language developing project that I had put it as an aimed project in the future "World Leaders Education Institute", its outline is what I would like to recommend to you all. So, it was attached to the end of this book. And the position of the head of that language department is open. May be you can apply. Thanks.

The author, Feb. 2018
Dallas. TX, USA

www.ingramcontent.com/pod-product-compliance
Ingram Content Group UK Ltd.
Pitfield, Milton Keynes, MK11 3LW, UK
UKHW051134260726
13967UKWH00010B/3035

9 781387 584611